All About
Helen Keller

Chris Edwards

BLUE RIVER PRESS

Indianapolis, Indiana

Published by Blue River Press
Indianapolis, Indiana
www.brpressbooks.com

Distributed by Cardinal Publishers Group
A Tom Doherty Company, Inc.
www.cardinalpub.com

ISBN: 978-1-68157-096-9
Library of Congress Control Number: 2018905556

Author: Chris Edwards
Cover Design: David Miles
Book Design: Dave Reed
Cover Artist: Jennifer Mujezinovic
Editor: Dani McCormick
Illustrator: Amber Calderon

Printed in the United States of America

7 6 5 4 3 2 1   18 19 20 21 22 23 24

Contents

All About
Helen Keller

Preface

The world that Helen Keller lived in was dark and quiet until a woman named Anne Sullivan came into her life. Helen was just six years old in the 1880s when she and Anne had to find a way to work a miracle out in the countryside of Alabama. Anne Sullivan had to find a way to reach into the quiet world of a deaf and blind girl to teach Helen to see, hear, and communicate in a different way.

The story of Helen Keller and her teacher Anne Sullivan has been told over and over again. It is a story about how a teacher who would not quit helped a girl who could not see or hear. The story is an inspiration to people all over the world and it has made people look at the deaf and blind in a new way.

As she grew up, Helen Keller did not want to be just an inspiration. She wanted to be a smart woman who was respected for her ideas, not just a girl overcoming a disability.

Helen Keller was not just someone who made life better for the deaf and blind. She also helped make life better for other women. She advocated for women's health and demonstrated that women could write books. She argued that women should be able to vote during a time when that was not the case everywhere.

Students who learn in schools for the blind or deaf likely know a lot about Helen Keller. She was the first person who was deaf-blind to go to college. She was proof that deaf and blind people could be taught in the same schools that everybody else was taught in. Even though she could not see, she changed the way other people saw disability. Even though she could not hear, she could speak out.

The most famous part of Helen Keller's life was her childhood and relationship with Anne Sullivan. However, she was an important person for political reasons. At age seven, she met her first president, President Grover Cleveland. She later met every president after him, all the way up to Lyndon B. Johnson. President Johnson gave her the Presidential Medal of Freedom. It is the highest honor that an American citizen not in the military can receive.

Helen Keller made a lot of friends in her life. Alexander Graham Bell, who invented the telephone, knew Helen from the time that she was just a girl. They remained friends until his death. Helen not only knew Mark Twain, but the two shared a love of books and writing. Twain praised Helen's writing and thought of her as an important author.

The many plays, movies, and television specials made about her life provided an example of how people with disabilities should be treated. Helen's work with the American Foundation for the Blind (AFB), helped to expand the number of books made available to blind people. She became one of the most famous Americans in the world.

Still, Helen got lonely. Her circle of close friends never became very large because most people could not communicate with her. By the time she died in 1968, her mother, father, and Anne Sullivan had all passed away. Helen remained a bright presence up until the end, reading books and meeting with people. Her work made life better for the deaf-blind and helped gain more rights for women.

Although from very different backgrounds, Anne and Helen had an unbreakable bond for most of their lives.

Chapter 1
Helen's Childhood

Helen grew up on a rural cotton plantation in Alabama.

Helen Keller was born on June 27, 1880 in the town of Tuscumbia, Alabama. Her father, Captain Arthur Keller, had been a soldier for the South during the American Civil War. He had earned the title of "captain" while serving in the Confederate Army. Kate Adams, Helen's mother, married Captain Keller. She was in charge of taking care of the large number of houses and property that the Keller family owned. She also helped to raise Captain Keller's other children from a previous marriage. In addition to taking care of Helen and her half-siblings, Kate gave orders to the maids and cooks who worked on the large Keller property.

Kate Keller was the daughter of a Confederate general and a distant cousin of Robert E. Lee.

For the first year and a half of her life, Helen was a healthy baby. She crawled on the floor, cuddled with her mom and dad, and played with the other kids in the house. She learned how to ask for water by saying "wa-wa." Then, when she was nineteen-months old, she got very sick.

In modern times, most babies get vaccine shots against dangerous diseases. In 1880, however, these shots had not yet been created. It was common for kids to get sick, and they often died from these illnesses. The virus that made Helen sick gave her a very high fever. She got so hot that her mom became scared that Helen might die. For many days, Helen's forehead was almost too hot to touch.

Finally, the fever broke, but Kate Keller was still worried. Helen did not respond to noises or to anything that moved in front of her face. Kate waved her hands in front of Helen's eyes but got no response. She made noises around Helen, but the little girl did not act as if she heard anything. After a while, Kate and Captain Keller had to face the truth. Their daughter was deaf and blind.

Meningitis, what probably made Helen sick, was discovered in 1805, but the doctors in Alabama didn't know about it yet.

The Keller family had some money, so they took Helen to all of the best doctors in Alabama. None of the doctors knew what to do. They could not even figure out what had made Helen sick to begin with. They said that Helen had gotten brain fever, but modern doctors think that Helen might have had meningitis. Meningitis is a virus that infects the spinal fluid that goes to the brain.

As Helen started to grow up, she could still walk and run. She used her hands and fingers to learn about everything around her. She hugged her mom a lot for comfort. No one in the family knew how to talk to Helen, and she would often get upset because she couldn't communicate with anyone.

When Helen got upset, she would throw a tantrum. She would act wild and break things. Because of her tantrums, a lot of people outside

Helen loved animals because she didn't need language to communicate with them.

of Helen's family said that the girl was crazy. They said she should be sent away to live in an asylum with other crazy people. Helen was not crazy. She was just frustrated because she could only communicate with people by shaking her head for "no" or by nodding her head for "yes."

Sometimes the things that Helen thought were funny could be misunderstood and seen as mean. One time, Helen locked her mom in a room for three hours and giggled about it the entire time.

For the family, the worst time to be around Helen was at meals. The girl ran around the table and grabbed food from everyone else's plate. Helen would take bites out of the food to see if she liked the taste. If she liked the taste, she would eat the food. If she did not like the taste, she would put the food back on the plate with a bite taken out of it.

Kate and Captain Keller didn't know what to do with their daughter, so they just let Helen run wild. If they tried to control Helen, she would throw a tantrum, so they stopped trying to make her behave. Still, Helen's mom and dad loved her very much. Helen would play with her dad and sometimes helped him "read" his newspaper by putting on his glasses. She liked to grab her mom's skirts and walk around the house with her.

Helen also played with the other people in the house. She had one half-brother that still lived there, an aunt, and cooks and maids that came to be her friends. However, if Helen's behavior

Helen was well-loved by her family and their staff, and even developed a rough form of sign language to talk with them.

did not get better, it was not clear that she could stay in her home as she got bigger and older. Helen often got out of control. Her mom and dad hired many cooks and maids. These workers would bring their own kids with them to the Keller house. Helen would play well with the kids sometimes, but could also get angry very quickly and break the other child's toys.

For the first three years after she lost her ability to see and hear, the Keller family could handle Helen's actions. Things got worse as Helen got older and started to endanger the family. Once, she laid an apron over a fire and nearly burned down the house. Then, when Helen was five years old, her mom had another baby. Helen's baby sister was named Mildred. Their mother laid Mildred down to sleep in a cradle Helen liked to use for her best doll. When Helen found her baby sister in the cradle, she dumped Mildred out onto the floor.

Luckily, Mildred was just scared by the act and not badly hurt. Still, Helen was a danger to her new sister and no one in the family knew how to make Helen act better. If she could not behave, Helen would have to be sent away. Kate and Captain Keller began to look for someone who could teach Helen to act correctly.

Helen loved her younger sister, but had
a hard time communicating with her.

Chapter 2
Looking for Help

Kate Keller looked everywhere for a way to help Helen. In 1885, it was hard to find ways to help children with Helen's special needs. Very few children in the world were deaf-blind like Helen, so very few ways of helping kids like her had been created. Finally, Kate Keller read a book titled *American Notes* by the famous English writer Charles Dickens. In this book, Dickens mentioned a special school in Boston, Massachusetts that only taught students who could not see. The school was called The Perkins Institute. When he visited the Institute, Dickens met Laura Bridgman. Like Helen, this girl could not see or hear.

Dr. Samuel Howe at the Perkins Institute found a way to communicate with Laura. People who cannot hear usually talk to one another by making words with their hands in sign language. It works well for people who can see but cannot hear. Howe made a kind of sign language that could be used by students who could not see or hear. He signed the words into the palm of the student's hand, and over time she had learned how to talk with other people in this way. This became known as finger spelling.

By this time in Helen's life, Kate and Captain Keller began to see that Helen was a smart girl. She was coming to an age where she needed to be in school learning about new things.

The Perkins Institute for the Blind is the oldest school for the blind in the United States.

One of Helen's doctors sent the family to meet Dr. Alexander Graham Bell. Dr. Bell was an inventor who had created the first telephone in

1876. The invention of the telephone made Dr. Bell famous.

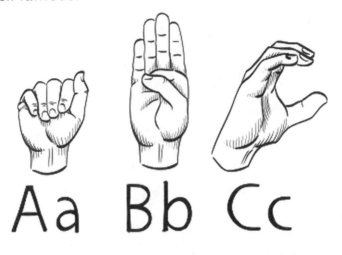

American Sign Language was adapted to English from French sign language.

Dr. Bell had a strong interest in education for the deaf. His mom could not hear and both of his parents were speech teachers. His invention of the telephone was just a small part of an entire life spent working with sound and hearing. Helen met Bell when she was just a small child and liked him right away.

They managed to talk using the crude sign language that Helen had made up. Dr. Bell saw that Helen could be a great student if she just had the right teacher. He told Captain Keller to write a letter to the people at the Perkins Institute telling them about Helen. The people at the Perkins Institute soon wrote back that they would send a teacher out to meet Helen.

Chapter 3
Anne Sullivan

Anne's full name was Johanna Masfield Sullivan,
but she was always called Anne or Annie.

Anne Mansfield Sullivan would be Helen's teacher. She was only twenty-years old when she was assigned to Helen, but her life had been hard and made her tough. She was ready to take on a challenge as difficult as trying to teach a deaf and blind child like Helen.

Anne could hear, but she could not see well. At the age of three, her eyes got infected and became itchy. The infection hurt her eyes, but her mom and dad did not have enough money to pay for a doctor to help her. The Sullivan family had to deal with both poverty and sickness.

After Anne was born, Anne's mother got sick with Tuberculosis, usually abbreviated to TB. In the 1800s, a lot of people in the United States got sick from TB. Tuberculosis is caused by bacteria growing in the lungs. People with TB get sick over a long period of time and usually die after several years.

Even though she was sick, Anne's mom had two more kids. Anne's brother, Jimmie, was born first. Jimmie had a bad hip that was likely caused by his mother's TB infection. Then Anne's mom had Anne's sister, Mary. Anne did not have a happy childhood despite her loving siblings. Anne's dad was an alcoholic which means that he was addicted to drinking alcohol and could not stop. Anne's dad got mean and violent when he drank too much.

Children made up one-third of the people at the Tewksbury Almshouse when Anne and Jimmie were sent there.

When Anne's mom died from TB, Anne's dad was not fit to take care of all the kids, so they had to live with other relatives. Anne could barely see, and her brother, Jimmie, could barely walk. The relatives thought that Anne and Jimmie were too hard to take care of. They kept the youngest kid, Mary, but sent Anne and Jimmie off to live in a poorhouse.

Anne, then ten years old, took care of her five-year-old brother. The poorhouse held many criminals and alcoholics, and bugs and rodents infested everything. Jimmie got sick and died while they were there. Anne lost her eyesight almost completely. After four years of living in the poorhouse, Anne met some visitors from the Perkins Institute. These visitors had Anne moved to their school for the blind.

Anne had lived through so many bad times that she had grown tough and independent. Still, she had never been to school. She could not read, write, or do math.

At the Perkins Institute, Anne learned how to use her fingers to read raised bumps on a page. The words were written in an alphabet for the blind called Braille. Anne worked hard and became smarter. For six years, she learned new things. It was amazing, but this girl who could not read, write, or do math at age fourteen, graduated from the Perkins Institute at the top of her class. She grew to love her school and its teachers. In 1887, Anne was only twenty-years-old when she received a letter asking if she would like to try to teach a young deaf-blind girl named Helen Keller. Anne said yes.

Braille is named after its creator, Louis Braille, who created the code at only fifteen years old.

Chapter 4
The Miracle Worker

PERKINS SCHOOL FOR THE BLIND

TUSCUMBIA

Anne, Helen, and members of the Keller family would become very familiar with the trip from Tuscumbia to Boston.

Anne Sullivan arrived in Tuscumbia in the late winter of 1887. She met Helen Keller at the Keller estate and wanted to get right to work teaching the girl. The difference between the well-kept Keller estate and Helen's appearance shocked

Anne. The Kellers were wealthy, but Helen looked like a girl from the poorhouse where Anne had spent so many years. Dirt streaked Helen's hair and she wore old, stained clothes.

The first meeting between Anne and Helen did not go well. Anne bent down to let Helen explore her face with her little hands. Anne's eyes hurt from the long and dirty train ride, but she could see the potential in Helen Keller. Anne tried to hug her new student, but Helen broke free.

Anne's plan was to force her pupil to behave. She would discipline the wild child and teach her through a method called finger spelling. Finger spelling is where the signs for letters and words are spelled into the palm of the hand of the deaf-blind person.

To get off to a good start, Anne had brought Helen a nice doll. Helen took the doll and became attached to it right away. Anne spelled the word "doll" into Helen's palms, but Helen did not yet see that the word was meant to stand for the real doll.

Anne did not fit in with the Keller family immediately,
but she bonded quickly with Helen.

Anne could not stand the wild way in which
Helen behaved. When Helen grabbed food off
of everyone's plate at mealtimes, Anne decided
that was enough. Anne smacked Helen's hands
if the girl tried to grab food. Anne even told the
rest of the Keller family that they should leave
the dining room so that she could teach Helen
some manners. Helen had finally met someone
who was as tough as she was wild.

Anne nearly gave up in those first few weeks.
Helen's family had not known how to help her
so Helen had been allowed to do whatever

she wanted all of her life. How is it possible, everyone wondered, to teach a child who cannot see or hear?

Helen's behavior would have to improve before it would be possible for Anne to teach

Though she couldn't see, Helen was aware of how she looked, posing for cameras and asking, "Do I look pretty?"

her words and letters. The poor girl was locked inside her own mind, unable to talk to anyone. She couldn't even think like everyone else because she could not form words in her mind. She did not know what colors or songs were.

The house where Anne and Helen lived together is now a museum of Helen's life.

Anne came to think that she could only really teach Helen if the girl was removed from her family so that the two could concentrate on learning. That way she would feel that it was not possible to go back to the old days when she could run as wildly as she pleased.

Captain and Kate Keller allowed Anne to move to a cozy house on their property. They tricked Helen into thinking that she had moved far away by moving the furniture in the little house around so that she would not recognize it.

The little house only had one bed, and Anne intended to sleep next to Helen. Helen hated this and fought for hours before Anne won and the girl finally went to sleep. Every time that Helen tested Anne, Anne won. Anne knew Helen could only be taught by someone she knew she could not boss around.

Anne and Helen fought over everything for a few weeks. Helen would not behave, and even Helen's mom and dad seemed to think that the situation was not working out. As the two fought, Anne kept spelling into Helen's hand. Helen craved this contact, and Anne was the only other person in the little house.

Helen's mom and dad came to see her every day, but they did not stay for long. If Helen did not behave, Anne would not touch her or write words into her hand. This scared Helen, and she begin to behave so that she could feel her teacher's fingers spelling into her palm again.

Nicknamed "Miss Spitfire" at Perkins, Anne used all of her willpower to tame and teach Helen.

Chapter 5
<u>Breakthrough</u>

After a month of working together, Anne began to lose hope. Maybe the human mind could just not learn without the sense of sight or hearing. Helen could be sweet in short stretches of time, but she still threw tantrums often, and Anne had to tough it out.

The biggest problem was that Helen had not yet made the connection between the words that Anne spelled into her palm and actual things in the world. She needed to have an "ah-ha!" moment to realize what Anne was trying to teach her.

On April 5, 1887, the first big connection happened. In the 1880's, people got their water from pumps attached to wells under the ground. Since there was no indoor plumbing in the houses yet, people had to go to the pump to get water. The pump and the water were also a good place to cool down since there was also no air conditioning. It was important to stay cool in the Alabama heat, and the pump was Helen's favorite place.

The water fountain moment was shown frequently in movies, plays, and drawings of Helen. Many showed Helen as being much older than she was.

Anne cranked the pump handle until cold water rushed out over Helen's hand and into a can. Anne then spelled the word "water" into Helen's palm. Anne pumped more water and spelled the word "water" again. Helen became very excited. She understood now! The word "water" stood for the cold and wet feeling that sprayed out over her fingers. Anne had broken into Helen's mind. Anne could teach Helen now.

Helen wanted to know the words for everything. She touched Anne; she touched the pump; she grabbed a handful of dirt. She wanted to know the names of her toys. She learned over two dozen words on that first day. Helen Keller was no longer a wild child who could not communicate. She was a student, and Anne Sullivan was her teacher.

Helen's wild behavior had been a result of her lack of sight and hearing. Before Anne, Helen could do nothing but feel and act. Now, she could "hear" through the palm of her hands.

Helen and Anne began a curriculum that involved finger-spelling, sign language, typing, and Braille.

Anne spent the summer teaching Helen words, and as Helen learned, she began to act better around her family and other people.

Progress had been made, but Helen still needed to learn how to read. Helen learned all of the letters of the alphabet by touching raised bumps on the flash cards that Anne had. These flash cards were used to educate blind students at the Perkins Institute. Now that Helen knew what it meant to have words spelled into her hand, this part came easier.

Anne would spell the letter into Helen's hand. Then she put the girl's fingers onto the flash cards so that Helen could learn the letters in the same way she had learned what the word "water" meant. It only took one day for Helen to learn all twenty-six letters of the English alphabet.

Helen loved to learn new things, and she had a willing teacher. Helen loved Anne like she was a second mother. Anne began to let her roam around outside, touching things, and learning words.

Helen investigated her world through her sense of touch, developing very sensitive fingers.

From the time Helen got up until the time she went to sleep, she could feel Anne signing into her hands. She was the only person in the world with whom Helen could talk on a regular basis. Anne grew to love her student deeply, and Helen's mom and dad treated Anne as if she was a member of the family.

Kate and Captain Keller could not believe how much Helen had changed. The girl who had once been so wild seemed calm and content. She wanted to learn all the time. The story was so amazing that American newspapers became interested in Helen and Anne.

Chapter 6
The Perkins Institute

Anne Sullivan worked for the Perkins Institute and was expected to write to her bosses to let them know how things were going with Helen. The person she wrote to the most was Michael Anagnos, but Anne did not really trust him.

By 1888, Helen Keller was seven years old and a very bright child. She had learned hundreds of words and had moved beyond seeing how words stood for objects. She had begun to understand that words could stand for feelings or ideas. She was still, however, a child, and she had missed several years of learning before Anne had been assigned to her. She was behind on her education.

Michael Anagnos wanted to make everyone aware of Helen and Anne. He might have wanted to get publicity for the Perkins Institute as well, so he embellished the story of Anne and Helen. He wrote about the student and teacher as if they were doing impossible things

Michael Anagnos was the Director
at the Perkins Institute when Helen attended.

and made Helen seem like a child with almost superhuman powers.

In the spring of 1888, Helen, Anne, and Helen's mother all made plans to take a trip to Massachusetts to visit the Perkins Institute. Helen had already become famous due to the newspaper articles that Michael Anagnos had written. Even the President of the United States, Grover Cleveland, wanted to meet Helen. Helen, Anne, and Kate all stopped and met the president in Washington, D.C. on their way to Massachusetts.

Dr. Bell had such an impact on Helen that she would later dedicate her first biography to him.

On their trip, Helen, Anne, and Kate also talked with Alexander Graham Bell, who was pleased with how well Helen and Anne had gotten along. Dr. Bell had been following Helen's story closely and wanted to make sure that the girl continued to learn.

When the group finally made it to the Perkins Institute, Helen fell in love with the school right away. She had never been on a trip outside of Alabama before, so everything was new and exciting. The school had toys and books that were specially made for blind people, so Helen could play and read all that she wanted.

There was an older woman at the Perkins Institute named Laura Bridgman. She was the

Laura Bridgman and Anne were friends
when they were both students at Perkins.

first deaf-blind student like Helen to attend the Institute. She had been the person that Charles Dickens had written about that made Kate Keller reach out to the Institute. Helen and Laura met, but Miss Bridgman was quiet and reserved. She liked to stay in her room and sew. Helen was outgoing and loved to meet new people and learn new things.

While they were at the school, Helen took a trip to the Atlantic Ocean and ran right in. She made so many friends and did so many things that, when they all returned home, Tuscumbia, Alabama seemed dull. Anne was bored with the little town as well, and her eye problem was getting worse. She made the decision to have an operation on her eyes so that she could see better.

The operation meant that Anne would go on another trip back to Massachusetts and go back to the Perkins Institute for a while. In the summer of 1889, Anne had her operation and got a chance to learn more things at the school. Helen took classes in Alabama on how to speak French sign language.

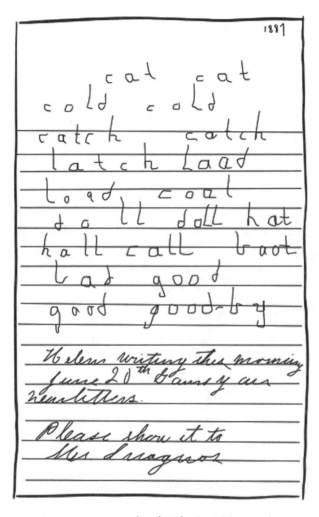

Anne sent a sample of Helen's writing saying,
"Helen's writing this morning, June 20th [1887].
G and Y are new letters. Please show it to Mr. Anagnos."

Helen could not see or hear, but this was not
always a disadvantage. Not being able to see or

hear meant that there were few things to distract her from learning. When she set out to learn something, it was all that she wanted to do. Her ability to concentrate let her learn new things very quickly. She picked up French sign language in just three months.

Helen learned more than just new words. She used her hands to learn about animals and to make arts and crafts. Her progress seemed amazing. Anne Sullivan's boss, Michael Anagnos, continued writing stories about Helen that embellished her abilities. Michael's stories made some people believe that Helen had become super smart, or that she was a genius with a special mind.

The truth was that Helen was simply a very bright child who loved to learn. She was just nine years old in 1890, but she was ready to take on a new and different challenge. She wanted to learn how to speak with her mouth.

Chapter 7
Becoming Famous

There were very few people in the world who could not see or hear like Helen Keller. Of those, one girl had learned how to speak verbally. So the teachers at the Perkins Institute knew that

Helen was not the only deaf-blind student at Perkins.
Shown here from left to right are Helen, Edith Thomas,
Elizabeth Robin, and Thomas Stringer.

such a thing was possible. However, no one at the Perkins Institute knew how to teach Helen because it was a school for the blind, not the deaf.

In Boston, there was a school for deaf students called the Horace Mann School for the Deaf. Teaching someone like Helen how to speak would be hard to do. But in the spring of 1890, the principal of the school, Sarah Fuller decided she would try.

Sarah Fuller did not spend as much time with Helen as Anne Sullivan did. Principal Fuller only gave Helen a few tutoring sessions so that Helen and Anne could practice on their own. During those sessions, Principal Fuller put Helen's fingers on her own throat and mouth so that Helen could feel the different vibrations associated with sound.

Helen worked hard and learned to speak well enough that her family could understand her. She had joined the world of sound even if she could not hear herself talk. Her mother and sister were overjoyed to hear the sound of Helen's spoken words.

Anne would read aloud to Helen to help her learn to speak.

The fame that Helen had earned had a downside. Michael Anagnos at the Perkins Institute kept writing stories for readers that were eager to hear more news about the miracle girl that he told them Helen Keller was. Helen was not a child genius, and she could not do many of the things that Mr. Anagnos wrote that she could.

To the public, Helen became a legendary deaf-blind girl who seemed to have a special power for learning new talents. Helen was so well-known that when she got caught up in a scandal, it blew up into big news. The scandal about Helen involved an issue with her own writing and Michael Anagnos.

Authors are not supposed to copy the work of another writer without giving the other writer credit for the work; it's called plagiarism. Helen read so many books that she lost track of the stories. One time, she sent a letter to Michael Anagnos at the Perkins Institute and included a small story that she had written called *The Frost King.*

Always eager for publicity, Anagnos wrote an article about Helen and included the little story that she had sent to him. The problem with this publication was that Helen's story seemed very similar to *The Frost Fairies* written by Margaret Canby. Helen was accused of stealing this story and passing it off as her own work.

To make matters worse, Anagnos had been exaggerating Helen's abilities for a long time. The incident with the story made it look like all of Helen's accomplishments had been fake.

Helen enjoyed the attention she received
for her accomplishments, but didn't enjoy being held
to such high standards.

Some people said that Helen was a fraud and
that Anne was really the smart one and just told
Helen what to do. Helen was only twelve years
old, and it is most likely that she had simply
made a mistake, but some people wanted to
believe the worst about her.

Anyone who knew Helen knew that she would not lie on purpose and the incident soon passed. The public was soon eager to hear more stories about Helen and her incredible ability to work hard and learn. Helen began to seek out other deaf-blind people. She wanted to help other people in the same way that Anne Sullivan had helped her.

Helen loved animals, patricularly dogs, and often traveled with them.

Helen began getting invited to attend big events and even got to attend President

Rutherford B. Hayes's inauguration. As Helen became a teenager, she spent more and more time studying and reading. She developed a love of animals and seemed to enjoy doing any activity that could keep her fingers busy.

As Helen grew up, her friendship with Anne Sullivan grew stronger and the pair spent a lot of time together. Helen simply called Anne "Teacher." Helen's love of learning, however, meant that she had to seek out other teachers in subjects that Anne could not teach her, like Latin.

By the time that Helen was fourteen years old, she needed to attend a more advanced school. Helen's father was no longer rich, so Helen had to rely on wealthy people who believed in her to pay for her to go to school. Although no record exists as to when Helen first met the wealthy philanthropist John P. Spaulding, she became very close with him over the years. The two wrote several warm letters to each other. Mr. Spaulding offered to pay her tuition to a new school.

Helen wanted to go to the Wright-Humason School for the Deaf in New York. Helen's goal at her new school was to learn how to speak in a totally "normal" way so that anyone listening to her voice would not suspect that Helen was deaf. Helen wanted to be able to talk to large groups of people about her life.

Upon her graduation from Wright Humason, Keller could read lips, speak, sign, and fingerspell in three languages.

Not only did Helen learn to speak to other people, but she learned a new way to listen to other people. Some people who can see but not hear can learn to read lips. Since Helen could not see, she had to read lips using her fingers. She learned how to put her fingers on the mouth of another person while that person spoke and "listen" through her fingers.

Helen had been inspired by Dr. Alexander Graham Bell's belief that deaf and blind people could learn how to live and communicate in a world full of seeing and hearing people. She wanted to be able to mix with other people, make new friends, and share ideas. Learning to read lips with her fingers was one of the hardest things that Helen ever tried to learn how to do. As always, she kept working until she figured out how to do it.

New York is a long way from Alabama, but Helen liked it in New York because something new was always going on. As she got older, Helen began to think about going to college. The once-wild little girl was now an educated and famous young woman. She was eager to go to college so she could continue learning.

In 1895, Helen met the famous American author, Mark Twain. They had lunch together in New York and became fast friends. Twain treated Helen like an equal, and she later wrote that she liked him so much because he did not treat her like a person with disabilities. Twain thought

Anne and Helen would read wherever they could, including in a tree with Helen's terrier Phiz.

Helen was very smart and pledged to give her money for her education. Twain and Helen both liked animals and traveling. Their friendship continued for the rest of Twain's life.

In 1896, while Helen was still in New York, she learned that her friend John P. Spaulding, who had paid her tuition, had died. Not long after this, Helen learned that her father had died. Captain Arthur Keller had always tried to do what was best for his daughter and Helen loved him deeply. The news of Captain Keller's death sent Helen into a long period of sadness.

Chapter 8
Going to College

Now that Helen was preparing for college, she ran into a problem. Up to this point, her education had been about learning how to communicate with other people. She read books, but had not gotten a serious education in the core subjects of math and science. Helen had worked her whole life just to develop communication skills that came naturally to most people.

Radcliffe College was the all-female version of Harvard College's all-male school. They officially united in 1963.

Helen wanted to attend the all-girl Radcliffe College in Cambridge, Massachusetts, which was a top school like Harvard University. In order to get herself ready for Radcliffe, Helen attended the Cambridge School for Young Ladies, a school just outside of Boston.

Once again, Helen's fame, personality, and family connections helped her. A rich woman who was interested in helping Helen paid for her school. Her new teachers were not trained to work with deaf and blind students, so they all had to adapt their lessons for her by learning to "speak" with their fingers into the palm of Helen's hand.

Very few books were published in the raised-bump format of writing known as Braille. This meant that Anne had to "read" books into the palm of Helen's hand. Helen had to try to memorize much of the content she learned in class so that she could make use of it at a later time.

The Cambridge School for Young Ladies proved to be a real challenge for Helen. She had an interest in languages and learned them quickly, but she had grown to be a young woman without learning how to do math well. Trying to learn numbers and how to use them in different types of calculations is hard for almost everyone. For Helen, who lived in a world without sound or light, math was painfully hard to learn.

Helen read and reread the Braille books she had, but was upset that there weren't more available.

Helen's younger sister Mildred also came to attend the school. It was nice for Helen to have her sister and teacher with her at school, but Helen wanted to make friends with the other students as well. However, Helen's fame made her stand apart, and the other girls her age simply did not know how to talk to her.

Anne still could not see well. The infection she had in her eyes as a child had never fully healed. The long hours spent with Helen wore out Anne's eyes and mind. Anne was tired and lonely. Her life had been hard, and now she was in a place where most of the girls and teachers came from a wealthy background. She did not fit in. She was tough, smart, and determined, but she sometimes forgot her manners. This shocked people at the Cambridge School for Young Ladies.

Anne's toughness and dedication had once saved Helen from a life of quiet and darkness. But now Anne's high standards for Helen seemed to be driving Helen into a state of despair. Helen got sick often, and the principal of the school became concerned. He thought that Anne was too driven and emotional to take care of Helen anymore.

The principal, Arthur Gilman, may have been more concerned that a person from a poor background like Anne did not fit in well at a place like the Cambridge School for

Young Ladies. It was a well-respected school for the daughters of wealthy families. In the end, he was the principal at an important school, and Anne was just a tutor to Helen. His words and opinion carried great authority. When he asked Helen's mom to give him full legal custody of Helen, Kate Keller said yes. The principal told Anne that she should leave.

Anne was partially blind and had to read all of Helen's text books to her, straining her eyes more.

Anne Sullivan walked into Helen's life when the girl was deaf, blind, and wild. Anne was forced out of Helen's life when Helen was comfortable at one of the finest schools in the country. At the Cambridge School without Anne, Helen had no one but her sister, Mildred. Helen cried a lot and missed Anne.

Anne also soon became very sad without the company of Helen and Mildred. Finally, Anne got tired of being sad. She charged back to the school and demanded to see her student. The principal could not get Anne to listen to him. Anne would not leave without Helen, so he finally gave in.

Kate Keller then came to Massachusetts to visit her daughters and saw the effect that the whole ordeal had on Helen, Mildred, and Anne. She hired Anne back as Helen's teacher and took Helen and Mildred out of the Cambridge School for Young Ladies. The Keller family had friends in Massachusetts, the Chamberlin family. Helen, Anne, and Mildred all went to live with the Chamberlins and were treated just like family.

Cambridge School for Young Ladies was founded
by the same people that founded Radcliffe College.

While living with the Chamberlins, Helen
continued learning from Anne and a private
tutor. In this way, she earned her way into
Radcliffe College by passing the same exams in
language and math that students with normal
sight and hearing had to pass. A lot of well-
known colleges accepted Helen, but she wanted
to attend Radcliffe more than any other school.

In 1900, Helen Keller was twenty years old.
Her acceptance to Radcliffe College made
history. No deaf-blind person had ever gone to
college in all of history. Still, the professors and
administrators at Radcliffe were worried about

rumors that they had heard about Helen and Anne. For a long time, some people had thought that Anne was like a puppet master, and Helen was her puppet. The people who spread these rumors thought that Anne Sullivan was very smart and did Helen's work for her.

In order to prevent any cheating, Radcliffe's professors put a lot of rules in place to make sure

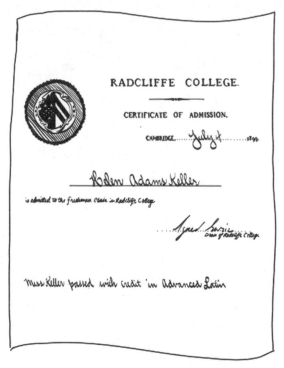

Helen was the first deaf-blind person to go to college.
No one else would go for another 50 years.

that Helen was the one who took the tests and not Anne. Helen would be watched while she took tests, and her attendance to class would be carefully monitored. Helen did not mind this, but she came to dislike Radcliffe. Helen was very sociable. She liked to be around people and wanted to make friends with the other young women at the school. She could not do that at Radcliffe because the other girls found it so hard to talk to her. It often seemed that only Anne knew how to communicate with Helen and this limited Helen's social life.

Also, the amount of work and studying required to do well at a famous school like Radcliffe was overwhelming. Helen could barely keep up and spent every spare moment studying. Helen's best subject had always been English, and at Radcliffe she found a chance to get better at writing. In 1902, Mark Twain read about the incident involving Helen and *The Frost King* from ten years earlier. He leapt to her defense. He said that what she had written was not plagiarism but a creative rethinking of something that Anne had read to her about. With America's best author on her side, Helen felt ready to write for the public.

Helen studied during all of her free time in order to keep her grades up, but she regretted not having friends to socialize with.

Chapter 9
Becoming a Writer

Helen was actually very good at typing, even better than Anne.

Helen's professors helped her learn to write well. So well, in fact, that she thought she might like to write a book of her own. A popular women's magazine called the *Ladies' Home Journal* paid Helen to write a history of her own life for their readers in multiple articles. Helen got help from an editor named John Macy. John was smart, young, and good-looking, and caught Anne Sullivan's eye while he helped write Helen's stories for the magazine. In 1903, the magazine stories were published together in a book titled *The Story of My Life*.

Helen graduated Radcliffe with honors and very good grades.

The first sentence of the book reads "It is with a kind of fear that I begin to write the history of my life." Helen then wrote that she was afraid that she would not really be able to remember her childhood. She had learned so much and talked with so many people for so long that she did not think she could recall how things had been so long ago when her mind had been so different.

Not long after her book's publication, Helen finished school at Radcliffe. She had earned a diploma from one of the finest schools in the United States and gained special honors from Radcliffe as a top student. She also met President Theodore (Teddy) Roosevelt. Roosevelt liked Helen's toughness and later wrote her a letter saying how much he enjoyed her book.

Helen soon found out that John Macy and Anne Sullivan were in love. The two had spent a lot of time together while John helped Helen get her book ready to be published. John and Anne asked her if she would mind if they got married. Helen replied that she thought that they should.

After Anne and John got married, Helen moved in with them and they all lived together. Helen was now a well-educated woman in her mid-twenties and enjoyed talking with John. In addition to being her editor, he was also a good friend and someone who knew how to communicate with Helen. Politics at this time was a big topic and John, Anne, and Helen often talked about politics and world events.

Helen, John, and Anne often discussed politics.

For several decades, a group of thinkers called socialists had argued that society was unfair. In the year 1848, a German writer and socialist named Karl Marx published a small pamphlet with his friend Friedrich Engels. It was called *The Communist Manifesto*. Marx said that the working class people of the world should take over and make things equal for everyone.

Karl Marx's views created a new way of looking at power in society. This was called Marxism.

Helen had lived with handicaps, and Anne Sullivan had lived through awful poverty. So both women liked to side with people who needed help. John Macy talked a lot about the work of Karl Marx and other socialist thinkers, and Helen quickly became fascinated by this. For a long time, Helen had been a Christian and a believer in the idea that everything would be made fair in the afterlife. But socialism promised to make things fair in this life. She believed in both Christianity and socialism for her entire life.

Helen used her skills as a writer to publish articles about improving health care for women and the poor. Helen also thought that workers should get more money from the people who employed them. At the same time that she became interested in making life better for the poor, Helen became interested in women's rights as well. Helen joined the socialist party in 1909. She wanted the world to change.

In that year, she went to see her old friend Mark Twain where he lived in Fairfield County, Connecticut. Twain was in the last year of his life, and the two had their picture taken together several times. Twain praised Helen's book. He died in 1910, but the words he wrote in a 1903 letter to Helen would become famous later. In that letter, he had called Anne Sullivan a "miracle worker."

Mark Twain said that the two most interesting people to come out of the nineteenth century were Napoleon Bonaparte and Helen Keller.

In 1909, most women in the United States could not yet vote. Each state could make its own laws about women's voting, but only four states let women vote equal to men. Women across the country were upset by this and started protesting that every state should let women vote.

The United States Constitution is the law for every state in the country. If the Constitution does not mention something specifically, the state governments get to decide what is best for the state. For example, the Constitution does not say anything about speed limits for cars, so each state sets its own speed limits. However, if a law is in the Constitution, every state has to follow it.

In 1909, only some states allowed women to vote. Many restricted their voting to certain elections.

The Constitution didn't say anything about women voting, but it is possible to add to the Constitution by amending it. That was what the suffragettes wanted to do. If the Constitution included a law that said that all women could vote, then every state in the country would have to follow the law. Helen joined the suffragettes in protesting for the right to vote. Eventually they were successful, and in 1920, the nineteenth amendment was added to the Constitution, giving men and women both the right to vote.

At the same time, Helen began trying to live by her socialist ideas. She did not want to take money from rich people who did not share with everyone. She continued to advocate for the blind. She met with President William Howard Taft at a ceremony to open a "lighthouse," a community and education center, for the blind in February of 1913.

Helen also wrote a new book about politics in 1913, but very few people read it, which hurt Helen deeply. She had become famous and well-educated because of her disability, but she wanted to be seen as a respected thinker who fought for social justice. Because of her first book, most people already thought of Helen as girl with disabilities and could not see her as a woman with ideas.

"The nineteenth amendment guaranteed that women could not be denied the right to vote based on their sex."

Helen needed to make money. She would not take money from others, and her books were not selling very well, so she had to think of some other way to bring money in. She figured she could make money by speaking at events. Anne decided to help Helen, and they both would speak to large crowds and answer questions from the audience.

Anne's health was not good. Her eyes hurt a lot, and she was often sad. Her husband, John, was not home very often, and Anne missed him. When Helen and Anne spoke to crowds, not many people showed up, and they did not make much money. Things got so bad that Helen had to start accepting cash from rich donors for a while. Finally, she and Anne decided to try going on a speaking tour again, but this time they hired people to market it.

Helen's lectures to crowds were a big hit this time. Lots of people came to hear her talk, and she was well-known across the globe. The world, however, was moving towards war. At the same time, Helen found out that Anne was very sick. The doctors diagnosed Anne with tuberculosis.

Chapter 10
Love and Loss

Helen hired someone to replace her sick friend and help on the speaking tour. His name was Peter Fagan, and he soon fell in love with Helen. By this time, Helen was in her thirties, but Peter was her first boyfriend. Helen's mother and Anne thought that people with disabilities should not have normal romantic desires. Helen's mother had spent a lot of effort to keep Helen from

Peter Fagan was a reporter hired to be Helen's personal secretary while Anne was sick.

ever being alone with a man during her life. At one time, Helen's mother even required that a man overseeing Helen's exam be changed for a woman.

For a long time, Helen had been curious about the opposite sex, and she fell quickly in love with Peter. Despite their love for each other, Peter insisted that they keep quiet about their relationship. Helen's mother was not likely to approve of Peter because he was not from a wealthy or well-known family. The couple filed for a marriage license in secret. Since a marriage license is part of the public record, a Baltimore newspaper reporter found out about the license.

Helen's mother believed that should not have romantic relationships because of her disabilities. However, if she were going to have a relationship, Kate Keller wanted it to be with someone of the same social standing. Helen was from a wealthy Southern family and had attended one of the best schools in the country. Peter was just a secretary. To Helen's family, honor and social standing mattered a lot. At one point, Helen's brother-in-law, Mildred's husband, pulled a gun on Peter and told him to keep away from her. The family forcibly took Helen to Mildred's house in Alabama.

Helen was a grown woman and felt as if her family had always treated her like a child who needed taking care of. She wanted to be with Peter. Helen had friends who agreed that she should be allowed to marry Peter, and they helped the couple send love letters back and forth. In this way, Peter told Helen that they would sneak off to get married.

Helen wanted to marry Peter and to escape the paternalistic treatment of her family. They agreed on a time when they could meet, and Helen packed her things. In the quiet of the night, she snuck out with her suitcases and waited for Peter. She waited to feel his hands. She waited for him to kiss her. She waited for him to come and rescue her from her restrictive family.

She just kept waiting. Peter Fagan never showed up, and Helen never received anything from him again. The letters they had mailed to each other were later destroyed in a fire.

Soon after this heartbreak, Anne recovered from her illness. It turned out that her sickness had been misdiagnosed, and she did not have tuberculosis. The two women were back together again. The great global war that would later be called World War I started in 1914. The Germans attacked a little country called Belgium on their way to invading France.

Helen wanted to speak out against war, but she had to be careful. She and Anne needed money, and silent movies had just been invented. A movie about the two women might make money if the public did not consider them to be too politically outspoken.

Helen met with President Woodrow Wilson, but she did not like him very much. Wilson was a southerner like Helen, but he was not friendly like her. President Wilson tended to take any criticism of his political decisions in a personal way. He had gotten the United States into WWI in 1917, which Helen opposed, and he was cold to Helen when she visited. Nonetheless, Helen was polite to Wilson when she spoke and wrote to him, but she continued to carefully speak out publicly against the war.

Helen Keller was so famous that one of the very first movies ever made by Hollywood was about her and Anne. Despite her political beliefs and public speaking, most people still knew Helen Keller from her first book. The public still thought of her as an inspirational person who had overcome handicaps.

The movie about Helen and her life, *Deliverance*, did okay at the box office, but did not make much money for Helen and Anne. Still, Helen found that she liked to be in the public eye. She liked to be well-known and wanted to try acting on the stage. Anne and Helen went on the road with a vaudeville act.

Vaudeville was a type of stage show that included dancing and jokes. Anne still was not very healthy, and the stressful life of a traveling actress made it worse. She was not as social as

Helen and did not enjoy acting, even though the two were making money with the shows.

Helen's vaudeville act named her the
"8th Wonder of the World."

In the late fall of 1921, with World War I over, Helen got two pieces of awful news. She learned that her mom and her old friend Dr. Alexander

Graham Bell had both died. Helen bel
strongly that she would see her mom and L
Bell in Heaven someday, but that did not stop
her from being sad.

Also, Anne seemed to be getting sicker. She
did not have TB, but she was often sick, and she
could just barely see. Their vaudeville act had
grown stale, so the two went back to giving paid
speeches. Anne was not in good enough health
to keep traveling; Helen would need to find some
other way.

Soon, Helen started working with the
American Foundation for the Blind (AFB). Helen
liked the AFB's goals. The AFB fought to make life
easier for the blind, and wanted blind people to
have better chances to get educated, read books
in Braille, and find jobs. Helen's fame helped the
AFB to raise money and talk to politicians who
could help to make changes in laws.

Meanwhile, Helen started writing again.
Her political books had not sold well, so Helen
thought that another book about her life might
do well. She worked with an editor to write a new

her life that picked up where her last
t off. Also, Helen decided to write
religion. She had long believed in
where everything was made equal,
and she would be able to see and hear. She
also hoped to see her dead friends and family in
this afterlife.

Helen typed her manuscripts on both
a Braille and a standard typewriter.

By 1929, Helen's two new books were out for sale, and President Calvin Coolidge met with Helen. President Coolidge was Helen's opposite; she was outgoing and talkative, he was rather quiet. He did seem to like her quite a lot despite this. She was one of the few visitors who made him smile, and he wrote to her that "you have a wonderful personality and I'm glad to meet you."

Helen later talked President Coolidge into donating to the AFB.

Then the stock market crashed and caused the Great Depression. The Depression hit the United States very hard, and lots of people lost their money and jobs. Anne had hardships of her own. She lost her right eye in 1929. She had been in a lot of pain, and the eye was infected and so strained that Anne could not see out of it so, her doctors took it out. Anne could barely see out of the remaining eye, and she became very sad. Her husband, John, had moved out, and Anne never saw him anymore. This had been her only close relationship with anyone other than Helen.

By today's psychological definitions, Anne Sullivan would probably be considered severely depressed. She became so depressed that it was hard for her to function, and she would not travel with Helen anymore. Helen had to find a new person to help her talk with people again. This time, she chose Polly Thompson. Polly helped Helen talk to the United States Congress on behalf of the AFB. Congress decided to spend money to increase the number of books written in Braille for the blind.

Polly was hired to replace Peter Fagan
as Helen and Anne's secretary.

In 1930, Helen was fifty years old and in great health. She traveled through Europe and gave frequent speeches for the AFB. She was happy in her role as an advocate for the blind and with her success as an author and speaker. She met another president, Herbert Hoover, and was even getting invited to countries in Europe to speak about the importance of education for the blind.

Hoover was not one of America's most popular presidents because he was in office during the Great Depression. However, he was a caring man who worked to help the poor and disabled in his personal life. He worked with Helen to develop the Foundation for the Overseas Blind, which expanded Helen's influence even further.

Unfortunately, Anne Sullivan was not doing as well as Helen. Her hard life weighed on her, and she was very sad about losing her ability to see. Her husband, John, had not been around for a long time. In the early twentieth century, married couples could not easily get divorced, so sometimes married people just moved away from each other instead. In 1932, Anne and Helen found out that John Macy had died.

By 1933, everyone could tell that Anne did not have long to live. Her mental and physical health were both consistently poor. She worked with a writer to have the story of her own life published in a biography. She continued to get sicker and sicker. In the fall of 1936, she was down to her last few breaths of life.

Anne had spoken with her fingers into Helen Keller's hands for over fifty years by this point. It was only right that Anne died with her hands being held by those of her famous student. For a long time, Anne had watched as Helen gained honors as the first deaf and blind person to do many things. But now it was Anne's turn to do something first. She was the first woman to be laid to rest in the National Cathedral in the nation's capital.

Other women now buried at the Cathedral include President Ulysses S. Grant's granddaughter and President Woodrow Wilson's wife.

By the time of Anne's death, Helen had already found a new life as an advocate for people with disabilities. In 1932, Franklin Delano Roosevelt (FDR) became the first disabled president of the United States. He had lost much of the use of his legs as a young man due to a disease called polio. Polio is no longer a problem in the United States because of vaccines. But at one time it made many people sick and often led to the loss of a person's ability to move some of their muscles.

FDR said that learning to live with polio had helped to build his character. The entire country could see that it did not take away his energy for politics. FDR's wife, Eleanor Roosevelt, was active in politics and was much better known to the public than the first ladies who had come

Helen had a corsage made special for Eleanor to wear on the day of FDR's inauguration as president.

before her. For a lot of disabled Americans, FDR was a symbol of what could be achieved. For a lot of women, Eleanor Roosevelt was an inspiration.

The Great Depression continued to hurt the economy of the United States, so FDR and Congress created new laws and programs. These were supposed to make life better for people who were out of work or had disabilities. Helen used her fame and influence to advocate that blind people should be considered disabled for all legal purposes. When FDR put the Social Security act in to law in 1935, blind people were listed as "disabled" and could get benefits from the government.

After Anne died, Helen traveled to many places to avoid her sorrow. She was invited to Japan and decided that she and her new assistant, Polly, should go. At the time, Japan was acting very aggressively toward other nations, and the Japanese government tended to think of the United States as its enemy. Despite this, Helen was well-liked by the Japanese people and treated like a friend everywhere that she went. FDR saw Helen as an important ambassador to Japan.

When Helen got back to the United States, she published a small book about her travels. She had enjoyed Japan and helped improve relations between the United States and Japan

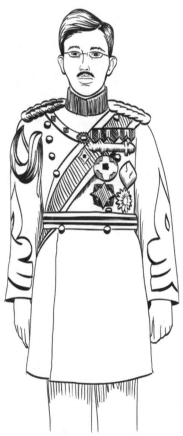

Emperor Hirohito invited Helen to the Imperial Cherry Blossom Viewing Party, a very famous party in Japan.

considerably. Helen was living in a comfortable home in Connecticut with Polly and working for the American Foundation for the Blind when World War II broke out.

In Germany, the Nazi party was in control of the country and led by a dictator named Adolph Hitler. The Nazis wanted to make Germany better by getting rid of everyone they thought of as undesirable. To do that, they purposefully killed many groups of people including socialists, Jews, and homosexuals. One of the first groups the Nazis began killing, however, was disabled people. On September 1, 1939, the German Army invaded the country of Poland and began killing people there, starting WWII. Helen was against most wars, but like a lot of people, she saw that Hitler had to be stopped.

The United States did not enter World War II for two years. But on December 7, 1941, the Imperial Japanese Navy Air Service bombed an American Naval base at Pearl Harbor in Hawai'i. FDR and the US Congress had no choice but to declare war against Japan and their ally Germany.

The bombing of Pearl Harbor is known as "A day that will live in infamy" from FDR's speech following the attack.

Helen was shocked and saddened by the Japanese attack on Pearl Harbor. She had come to like and admire people from Japan and could not believe what had happened. Helen saw that she had a role to play during the war and once again went into action.

The US entry in WWII meant that thousands of men came home from the war with serious injuries and disabilities. Helen spent a lot of time visiting with soldiers who had been made blind or deaf or given other injuries by the bombs and bullets of WWII. The rest of her time was spent

writing notes for a long book about her life with
Anne Sullivan.

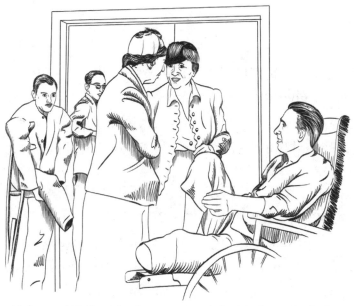

Helen and Polly visited veterans and disabled people during
WWII to raise spirits and promote courage and optimism.

Chapter 11
An Inspirational Life

When the war ended in 1945, Helen continued working for the AFB and went all around the world giving speeches and meeting with people. She was making people everywhere see that the deaf and blind could also be friends and workers.

One year after the war's end, Helen suffered a tragedy. Her house in Connecticut caught fire. The book she had been working on about Anne went up in flames. She handled the news with courage; after all that she had been through, losing a home did not seem like so much.

In 1954, Helen was the subject of another movie. This would be a documentary about her life and was called *Unconquered*, or sometimes just *Helen Keller in Her Story*. It won an Academy award, known as an Oscar, in 1955 in the category of Documentary Film.

Helen Keller is the only person to win an Oscar
for a documentary of herself and have
someone win an Oscar playing her.

After meeting President Dwight D.
Eisenhower, as she had many presidents before
him, Helen developed a close personal friendship
with him. In June of 1955, he wrote her a letter
for her 75th birthday, saying:

"Dear Miss Keller:

Please accept my warm congratulations on your forthcoming seventy-fifth birthday. The story of your accomplishments is not only a monument to your own great gifts of mind and heart. It is also an enduring inspiration—in many lands—to those who suffer physical handicaps and to those who seek to help the disabled toward richer lives. With all who honor you, I am glad to join in best wishes and in the hope that future years will bring you happiness."

A playwright named William Gibson had taken an interest in the story of Anne and Helen and wrote a play about the Helen's life. The play was called *The Miracle Worker* and came out on Broadway in New York City in 1959. It was performed over seven-hundred times and did not stop showing until the summer of 1961.

In 1962, a movie version of the play was made and became a huge hit with critics. It did not make a whole lot of money compared to some of the other movies but was nominated for five Academy awards. Anne Bancroft won the Best Actress award for playing Anne Sullivan. Patty

Duke won a Best Supporting Actress award for playing Helen Keller.

Helen and Patty Duke got to know each other quite well and Patty liked Helen a lot. Helen was eighty-two years old when the movie came out.

Patty Duke is the only actress to win an Oscar with only one word. In *Miracle Worker*, she says, "Water!"

The next year, in 1963 she had a stroke. Helen also became diabetic, which meant that she would have to keep track of her blood sugar levels.

She was now too old and ill to travel anymore. She had lived through so much, been to so many places, and met so many people, that Helen decided it was time to rest. She read books and talked with visitors and was happy to live the quiet life even as the United States went through dramatic changes in the 1960's. Helen did meet with President John F. Kennedy (JFK) and was particularly fond of his three-year-old daughter, Carolyn. This meeting was recorded for television cameras, and Helen can be seen laughing and joking with the president.

After JFK was killed by an assassin, Lyndon B. Johnson became president. President Johnson

While giving the award, President Johnson said, "An example to all mankind, [Helen] has devoted her life to illuminating the dark world of the blind and handicapped."

wanted to meet Helen, too. Helen was used to meeting presidents and did not think this was unusual. President Johnson, however, wanted to give Helen something special. The highest honor that can be given to a United States citizen who is not in the military is the Presidential Medal of Freedom. President Johnson gave this rare award to Helen Keller. Not long afterwards she was placed in the National Women's Hall of Fame.

These two honors made Helen Keller one of the most decorated and celebrated Americans in the world. It was amazing that a woman who could not see or hear had been able to speak so loudly that the entire world had heard her. In May of 1968, Helen had a heart attack. She lived on for a little while, but died on the first day of June.

The plaque for Anne and Helen's burial at the National
Cathedral includes the inscription in Braille.

Chapter 12
Helen's Legacy

Today, deaf and blind students have a choice. They can attend special schools for the deaf and blind. They can attend public schools with other kids who can see and hear. If a deaf student attends a school with students who can see or hear, then the school must have a person who can speak to the student in sign language. If the student cannot see, then the school must help that student to learn in ways that do not involve sight.

Also, schools now have to be accessible to wheelchairs so that people who cannot walk may be able learn. This was not always the case. During the time that Helen Keller grew up, it was hard for a deaf or blind person to go to school. People with disabilities could not always find a way to walk up stairs to get into schools. Helen Keller helped to change all of this by proving that deaf or blind people could do the same kinds of things that hearing and seeing people did.

Today, women can go to college and become anything they want. This was not always the case. During Helen Keller's life, women could not always get into college or find a job. For much of Helen's life, most women were not even allowed to vote or run for public offices. Helen helped to change this too.

USA
15c

HELEN KELLER
ANNE SULLIVAN

In 1980, the US Postal Service honored Helen and Anne with a commemorative stamp.

These are the big things that Helen is remembered for. She was more than just a public person. She had close friends, was a good person, tried to help people, and was friendly and outgoing. People who met her almost always liked her. She only worried about being deaf and blind when it made people reluctant to try and talk with her.

Modern doctors do not know for sure what disease made Helen become deaf and blind, but the condition she had is now called deaf-blindness. Almost no Americans now become deaf and blind during childhood because kids get vaccines to prevent most of the viruses that would cause deaf-blindness.

All of Helen's books are still in print and can still be found in libraries. For several generations, she was taught about in most of America's history classrooms. In 1995, the writer James Loewen wrote that "teachers have held up Helen Keller, the deaf and blind girl who overcame her physical handicaps, as an inspiration to generations of schoolchildren. Every fifth-grader knows the scene in which Anne Sullivan spells water into young Helen's hand at the pump."

Helen Keller caused controversy in her life. She was more than just a deaf-blind person who overcame difficulties. She took stands and changed laws. She inspired people, but she made them angry too. She was buried alongside her teacher Anne Sullivan in the National Cathedral, one of only four women to receive the honor.

Virtually everyone who encounters Helen Keller's story, is moved by what she was able to accomplish. The fact that society could never see Helen as more than an inspirational person cannot be blamed on her. It is also not Helen's fault that her own family never could see her as a free and independent woman who could make her own choices.

Helen Keller worked to break free of the constraints of her time period and advocated consistently for greater levels of freedom and access to education for women, the disabled, and workers. She proved that deaf-blind people, and others who are differently-abled, can achieve high levels of education if the right adaptations are put into place. This is her greatest legacy.

Helen Keller Quotes from
The Story of My Life (1903)

The most important day I remember in all my life is the one on which my teacher, Anne Mansfield Sullivan, came to me. I am filled with wonder when I consider the immeasurable contrasts between the two lives which it connects. (p. 12).

In reading my teacher's lips I was wholly dependent on my fingers: I had to use the sense of touch in catching the vibrations of the throat, the movements of the mouth and the expression of the face; and often this sense was at fault. In such cases I was forced to repeat the words or sentences, sometimes for hours, until I felt the proper ring in my own voice. My work was practice, practice, practice. Discouragement and weariness cast me down frequently; but the next moment the thought that I should soon be at home and show my loved ones what I had accomplished, spurred me on, and I eagerly looked forward to their pleasure in my achievement (p. 33).

I try to make the light in others' eyes my sun, the music in others' ears my symphony, the smile on others' lips my happiness (p. 71).

Helen Keller Timeline

1880, June 27   Born in Tuscumbia, Alabama

1882, January-February   Helen loses sight and hearing due to fever

1886, July   Helen meets Alexander Graham Bell

1887, March 3   Anne Sullivan becomes Helen's teacher

1887, April 5   Anne achieves a breakthrough with Helen at the water pump

1890, March   Helen learns to speak with her mouth from Sarah Fuller

1891   Helen experiences controversy over her short story *The Frost King*

1895   Helen first develops a friendship with Mark Twain

1896   Helen's father, Arthur Keller, dies

1903   *The Story of My Life*, Helen's autobiography, is published

1904, June   Helen graduates from Radcliffe College

1920, February   Helen Keller and Annie Sullivan star in a Vaudeville routine about their lives

1921   Helen's mother, Kate, dies

1923   Helen takes a position working for the American Foundation for the Blind

1929   Helen's second autobiography, *Midstream*, is published

1936   Annie Sullivan dies

1943   Helen helps the US at war by visiting blinded soldiers

World Timeline

1848 Gold discovered at Sutter's Mill, California

1850 California becomes a state

1869 Transcontinental Railroad opens

1871 The Great Chicago Fire

1876 First telephone call was made by Alexander Graham Bell

1881 The assassination of President James A. Garfield

1883 The Brooklyn Bridge opens

1886 The Statue of Liberty is dedicated

1889 Johnstown, Pennsylvania flood

1898 Spanish-American War begins

1900 Galveston, Texas flood occurs

1903 Henry Ford sells first Model A auto

1903 First airplane flight by Orville and Wilbur Wright

1906 San Francisco earthquake and fire

1914 Panama Canal opens

1917 US enters World War I

1920 First US commercial radio broadcast

1928 First commercially licensed TV station opens in US

1929-1939 The Great Depression

1931 Empire State Building completed

1932 Kidnapping of Charles Augustus Lindbergh, Jr.

1936 San Francisco—Oakland Bay Bridge opens

1937 Golden Gate Bridge opens

Helen Keller Timeline (cont.)

1946 Begins a tour of the world where she advocates for the deaf and blind

1959 *The Miracle Worker*, about Helen and Annie, debuts on Broadway

1965 Helen is inducted into the Women's Hall of Fame

1968 Helen Keller dies

World Timeline (cont.)

1941   US enters World War II

1946   First session of the United Nations is held

1955   US enters the Vietnam War

1965   Martin Luther King Jr. leads march from Selma, Alabama to Montgomery, Alabama

1968   Richard Nixon elected president

Glossary

Ambassador   A person sent to visit another country or group to represent another country or group

Confederate   In the Civil War, the states trying to leave the United States to form their own country

Crude   Rough or poorly planned

Depression   A mental disorder that includes sadness and loss of self-esteem

Fraud   A person who pretends to be someone or something they are not

Great Depression   A period of low business activity lasting from 1929 to 1939

Handicap   A problem or disadvantage that makes progress or success difficult

Meningitis   A disease that involves swelling of certain parts of the brain and fever

Paternalistic   Being very controlling of a person and wanting to oversee all parts of that person's life

Pearl Harbor   A major United States Navy base in Hawai'i that was attacked during World War II, killing many people

Philanthropist   A person who cares for other people, usually expressed through generous acts of kindness or charity

Plagiarism   Stealing someone else's ideas or words and saying they are your own work

Socialism   A system of government based on the idea of everyone sharing everything equally

Suffragettes   Women who wanted the right to vote equal to men

Union   In the Civil War, the states staying in the Unites States

Vaccine   A medicine, usually injected, that helps the body prepare for and fight off a disease

Bibliography

Garrett, Leslie. (2004). *Helen Keller: A Photographic Story of a Life*. London: DK.

Gibson, William. (1959). Reprint, 2008. *The Miracle Worker*. New York: Scribner.

Keller, Helen. (1903), reprinted 2004. *The Story of My Life: The Restored Edition*. New York: Modern Library Classics.

Further Reading

http://helenkellerfoundation.org/

Index

Index (cont.)

Index (cont.)

Index (cont.)

Index (cont.)

Index (cont.)

Index (cont.)

Index (cont.)

vibrations (in mouth), 40
viruses, 3, 4
voting (women's rights), 66, 67, 68, 69

W
water pump, 27
Wilson, Woodrow, 73
women's rights, x, 66, 67, 68, 69
words, learning new, 28
World War I, 73, 75
World War II, 87, 88
Wright-Humason School for the Deaf, 45, 46
writing, 37, 89, ix, viii
    about politics, 68, 69
    Braille, 78
    Keller, Helen, 59, 60–70
    Ladies' Home Journal, 60
    The Story of My Life, 61, 62
    Twain, Mark, ix, 47, 48, 58, 65, 66

All About... Series

A series for inquisitive young readers

If you liked this book, you may also enjoy:

All About Amelia Earhart
All About Benjamin Franklin
All About Edmund Hillary
All About Frederick Douglass
All About the Grand Canyon
All About Julia Morgan
All About Madam C. J. Walker
All About Martin Luther King Jr.
All About Roberto Clemente
All About Stephen Hawking
All About Steve Wozniak
All About Winston Churchill
All About Yellowstone

And coming soon:

All About the Appalachian Trail
All About Barack Obama
All About the Great Lakes
All About Mohandas Gandhi

Teachers guides and puzzles available at
brpressbooks.com/all-about-teachers-guides/